At the Bottom of the Year

Advent Poems
by
David Craig

Angelico Press

First published in the USA
by Angelico Press
© David Craig 2021

For information, address:
Angelico Press
169 Monitor St.
Brooklyn, NY 11222
www.angelicopress.com

pbk: 978-1-62138-784-8
cloth: 978-1-62138-785-5

Cover image: Linda Craig
Cover design: Michael Schrauzer

CONTENTS

PART II: BILLY COLLINS WALKS INTO WALMART TO BUY SOME HERBICIDE

PART I

Robert Bly Follows Jesus
into the Hay Barn

St. Catherine of Siena's Pazzo D'Amore
❧ for my Down's Brony son, Jude

The rest of us want this too: the movement that keeps
its place. We want to wave your wet asparagus
in the city square like aspergillum; we want

to use it to sprinkle the faithful: which would be anyone
close enough to reach. The people enjoy those tables,
the country wind that raises up some cloth.

This is how new days lead us: in fine vegetables,
in the reserve of those who quietly wait for a chance
to tell their goods. It's a happy education. We bite

the coins; they play the summer dust, the fields.
We long for the Name that creates us, the Holy Twitch
which pulls the strings of time. It's not our names

that'll be shouted throughout the squares. Our lives will bound
because He wakes fools—like me with my first
vision ever, this morning, an odd one: a plastic pink

toy horse, a unicorn! I saw it get up and dance!
So finish, Lord, what You've started! We're physical runes
on old Celtic crosses. We begin to twist in the ground.

Rump-a-Pum-Pum

Everything here is designed to get our attention:
garbage on Tuesday, which route to wheel it to the curb.
Nothing seems beneath our concern. Each blade

of grass must lift his frosted brothers! After all,
that's why we're here, isn't it? Our voices raised
in Dante's cacophony, so quiet that we can miss it.

"Sing ho, for the life of a bear." Christopher Robin
and Pooh march, "Sing ho, for the expedition!" Each wears
a new hat of some sort—maybe made of newspaper or foil.

We sing summer Christmas songs out the car window,
tell grazing Amish horses that Jesus loves them;
we come as we always have: alone, ill-equipped.

We have so little to lose. Everything before us:
a morning of invisible flowers, the day as it should be,
is. "Sing ho." I'm going Hawaiian this morning!

No one can stop me, a gesture God alone
can see. This is the only way to change
the world—beneath its surfaces, Pooh on parade.

Gene Kelly's Other Dance

Some days we feel our sodden plight, wet backyard
soaking our feet: nature, a cold blanket—
shelves of rock, jutting woods, the soil beneath,

how it conspires against itself. You can see that
in trees, a scramble of sticks; in our dog's "scrape
behavior" here in town as we walk, marring

a car with flying bits of mud and grass.
We try to restore its look. God lives, they say,
most clearly, in places like this: in a dark neighborhood,

early winter's perpetual drizzle. I don't doubt it, as we walk
down the street. Wet houses, lives, everything confesses
"Advent." I want to rip out a For Sale sign,

move it a foot to its left, though that wouldn't help.
The world, like our character, is intractable. It's a stone amulet.
It measures number, weight, and wet timber.

On some level we're like flapping geese—after effort
in the rain, the darkened roots are division, experience.
So we widen our leash, lengthen our dog's lead.

Kenneth Patchen in a Body Cast

Awash in his Albion moonlight, he spent his last thirteen
years on his back. His clothes, even there, suited
his form—one making commentary on the other.

He could have been a crucified angel, almost,
drops of living tin or rain; he had to have heard
the birds, mornings, as the sun flowered, rose up

over his neighbor's fence. How sorrow must've opened
him wide. (One does what he is made to do.)
Kenneth's bed was like two cymbals. It cracked

the dawn. He was wheeled into paradise. And even there,
he sneaks a crawl into his cast, that shell again,
just to see the birds fly straighter, the sun shed

surfaces. He cannot think of himself without it:
the plant goes back into seed, just to feel the shock
of origin. This helps him love everything. He doesn't

even have to talk to a person to know his story,
and each one makes him more completely himself.
Christ wears a body-cast on a necklace when they play bocci.

At the Intersection, Windows Down

Jude plays a July Christmas CD in the car.
And isn't God just like that, never changing
in the oddest ways? We're never where we were,

despite ourselves: an odd gift to anyone
close enough to bear us—our horn (or thorn) of plenty,
the flap of what might be angelic wings.

Why apologize for the madness? These are the noises
our skin makes as it outgrows itself. Hear the
green glass scratching—dark sheath, a lip! It's like someone

crying fire in a theater. Each of us is a warp-speed celebration.
My wife, for example, has so many arts she cannot
find the hours to persevere. And who would stay her hand?

We should face it. None of us owns a Christian house,
though we perch our statues. We should admit it: none of us
have mastered the time of day. And this is all

to the good. How else can we keep our doors open?
How else can He or others get into the fold?
We try to count while holding too many beans.

Inside the Boat

Who of us does not belong to the uneven black pitch,
the bead line inside this boat? Whose wrong-headedness
could calm the rolling axis of this granite world?

Our oarlocks are safe—with engraved name plates for
     everyone!
We all exist in tribes of one, not the greats.
(We left a thousand little oaken shields somewhere,

leather stuff, lying about, forgotten and glistening
in high grass, a morning of castle rain.) So what
is left us here? We might stand stout, claim lore.

I could Grump, my roots, strong boots for dwarves or trees.
(What I'm saying, friend, is I need to be there for you,
without the niceties! There's just too much at stake.)

Let there be an earnestness between us: that song we cannot
sing. Let us set our axes to wood, either living
or stacked. When I die, I want to fall, spent,

like John of the Cross, into the merciful chest of Jesus;
I want to wake slowly, so I can value new land.
Surrounded by wild turkeys, let me learn what I've missed.

English Dept. Minutes

I'm like a goldfish who keeps gaping at passing strangers,
looking for satisfaction as the world ignores me, good water,
as it goes its metalled ways—keenly, without

my direction! A parade of bi-peds, ground dwellers.
I don't know what to make of them, though the King
    occasionally
stops, taps on His aquarium glass. I startle

for a moment, but He's gone: that gentle beard, His approval!
I want to swim for Him, to circle the life-like
plastic plants. I want to learn everybody's name.

We are all bright swimmers here, valued for our color,
our splay; but for something deeper too. Our turns
sharpen! (The back wall seems to reflect more sun

after He passes.) He's the sea we swim in, St. Catherine
points out, a crown for our days. Watch us if you'd like!
You may admire yourself as we muse on program

adjustments, on endless ways to proceed. My boss
has wonderful hair; perhaps she could be a beta,
though she's much milder than that, enough to endure us.

Advent

Advent is like a very old door, much larger
than you, with burnished hinges, imported from old ships,
from lands before Atlantis. Every year it has to be opened—

not easily. The world is a cathedral in there, every person
has a place, a robe, a designation. The statues wait,
clothe the echoes. This world, like ours, is not

about us. It's like the Masses at the busy Vatican,
no one looks for your distant approval. The saints create
the nave, Our Lady's robe. They hold up each world.

This is the heart of God, Jesus: big and airy,
like the froth on your second Guinness, or the Scottish moors.
(Those with a door!) Here it's snow, and the year, beginning

its close: in sleigh-bells, in early, imagined night—
when love adopts the year. It's time to light
the fireplace, to open the real presents. It's time

for holy oil, for anointing young heads. We walk,
hills under late stars. It's cold outside, inviting;
you bundle, make footprints, under a crest of moonlight.

This Winter

Wet russet, that's the color of early winter:
old leaves and grasses at the base of trees, the shouldered
roads—blocking dwarven doors; and then

the great rises of blackened sticks, citizens
bending this way and that in their accumulated remorse:
what's left of snow—on this side of the year. It's nice

to drive through, though, to feel the distances. Winter is like
an old tambourine, barely music at all. It can wear
us down, and we're grateful for that. Everyone needs

the cuff of winter: a fiery barrel, where we
can find our icy hands; there's only circumference
enough to speak one heart—a want at a time.

Winter reduces each of us to grunts, to motion.
No daytime warehouse or recessed building invites
us home. This street, dirty snow, defies

TV reality, the lies we tell each other.
Take a bit of a pothole to bed—some coal for Christmas!
The cold creak of the bed will wake you early.

Hot Cross Buns

Gone, like corner bake shops, or our small-town mayor
who'd break a sweat with you under the pneumatic lift.
There's nothing you can count on anymore. On the other
    hand,

what is good keeps raising its green head under snow.
That's how angels have always gotten here in the first place.
They open your mind to possibility, and then they're eating

at your dining room table. "Pass the salt." "Watch
your sleeve." The gravy currents of give and take.
It's always some other that frees us up, isn't it?

It's the Jesus in them. We catch something of that place
where the two of them meet; we see all that they can be.
(Generosity has a face, but it's usually too hidden to see.)

We sometimes call it December, how the month closes up
around us, leaving us with so few options.
When there's only that one hearth, it draws many hands!

The fingers can warm, like faces opened to God—
or to us, the different sides of this world; like snow
in "The Dead," covering the plains: Joyce's Shannon.

Roethke's New Prayer
turning "My Papa's Waltz"

Winter rain: a reminder that we don't live here;
it's its own calling card, heavenly fingers
tapping on both sides of the window. Our answer

is to own this place. My wife does so with a chirp,
in over-alls; my daughter, too, whose smile helps
at the sink. It'll be that way, until time, its weathers

take us away from each other. We'll die in our beds,
each praying hard, sweating for the rest. We do
that now in our way, dancing around the place,

making jokes at the shaking plates. Even the dog,
who sneaks up, snout sideways after dinner. He's happily
himself, each of us, an audience and performer both!

We're like that one guy who claps at the back
of the theater. (It doesn't take much to get a rise
out of him! Life is spectacle which can only be had

in an act.) Let what's left to us be equipage for this play.
I'll hang onto my children, long after they're gone.
I'll play a pipe, as I try to right each wrong.

Breaking Acorns

The yellow trees are holding on. They bank
on their disposition. Because trees know why they stand—
choose not to move. (Someone has to point us home!)

Who knows what they discuss at night, the stars
webbing their dreams? In some ways it's better then.
The clear nights reduce you to who you are.

We are their bark, and the roots from which they spring,
though our home is in heaven. I want to hear them hear us:
the trees, my brothers and sisters. I would like to break acorns

together, to feel the rain make comment on our ridges.
(Our lives will be what will be revealed.) Daylight
will come, though it needn't. What wind could add to our
     store?

What rippling day-lit waters could give us a surer
skein? Our lives, these were never meant
for much. We pass along our leaves, a lesson

or two we learn out here in the dark. We pass
along His Name: the Many, though not by mouth,
never by mouth. The backs of our hands define us.

Wisdom Visits the Slow in Late Fall

The old yellow leaves flap for all they're worth;
the sun, farther along, but eager as always.
Though we change, the bright days of heaven never do.

They pass. Distracted, we don't particularly miss them—
like forgotten school children, we gather our books, pay heed
only to what happens in front of us, on the yellow ground.

That is where the table is spread, where friends reveal
themselves. It's where the rooster crows, Dylan
Thomas, with morning on his boyhood's bright shoulder.

Saints get made here: always two at a time,
though we never see the recipient. Still, anyone
within shouting distance is gathered into the fold!

Saints convert the countryside! We come at their voices.
(What we have, we owe. Who we are is someone else.
We're a creation largely authored by our betters!)

There's a rightness to this, more freedom than you would've
thought possible. We live at the King's ease, rejoice
at this world we've walked in on. (Everyone gets a chicken.)

The High School that Never Was

Another guy I didn't know died today.
People I didn't know too well mourned his loss.
So many of the living just pass me by. Great people,

from my high school class, from far off countries—France.
Mostly we get just bits of their goings-on.
These moments are tender, trade. (That small generosity

noted!) That's all we get of the next life, too.
We spend our days building a small fire. We crack
the kindling, find new room in our hearts. But that's it.

It was my loss not to know the man, nor the others
before him. Perhaps that's something we all must say.
(Good night, Tim! May flights of Jesuits sing you home.)

Jesus is all we know of this life, all we need to.
He died on a cross, ripped His skin to give us
a home. (The only problem is that it's not here.)

Here's to the glass I never got to raise, here's to
your loved ones, Tim—to the pain which made you whole.
May we, too, be happy fools, wherever the halls.

Naming Corn

Birds, morning, bring us around; they, and maybe
a walk along a stream; that will teach us calm
as they can be, though that feeling, too, passes.

We would like to change, rebuild our pasts; but that
would deny God His arc. We must grow out of what
we are. The sun, its clover, before time begins

to self-correct, to move horribly against itself:
all the faithful, bobbing slowly through long corn fields,
heading—somewhere. It often feels like that,

like we're pushing Simone Weil in a shopping cart
across a rutted field. Or is that when we're recently dead?
It doesn't matter. We won't even miss ourselves

because it'll be Jesus's fork, thrusting deep
into soil. We're peat, a scarf of land being turned
to make for better farm days. Too many of us tuning

banjos on a porch in the evening: a pack of third grade
teachers. We'll string flint, what we used to call Indian corn,
stars finally on our foreheads, giving up all we thought we
    knew.

The Best Days Pass

I would shine and be the new man, a pioneer of Truth.
I would be the crest at the family poker table.
But the truth lies elsewhere; we are the smallest of necessities.

We are not an answer one could use to recruit neighbors.
We give with no one knowing our face—not a
bad place in the end. The King of bottled beer,

the ice chest lives here. St. Francis would sit at our princely
picnic table. St. Therese would bring some guacamole,
a story or two from her convent days; their smiles,

deep-rooted, in the gut dirt of the place: what they favored.
Family quirks would own both of them in their way.
This is how the saints draw us out and into the world.

This is how heaven comes each time. In the mundane it carries.
Every friend is a backyard friend, every day comes
with a breeze. (You can set up a folding chair out there.

You can drink alone, take in the failing sky.)
Complain all you want about the problems in Washington;
the best days pass. The rest own the road news makes.

For Sam Cooke

We all get too full of ourselves, though most of us don't
have the money to create a headline. And so the sweetness
lies buried, and we're left with his voice, the gift he had

to give in the first place. He lies with the daffodils, those heralds
of spring, the diurnal course of rocks, skinned knees.
Like everyone, I'm sure he'd be happy to try again,

to heal the wounds he helped create. It's what
we do here, after all. One voice for Jesus at a time.
We walk in His wake. This is our honey. We're cave

people who paint our faces in starlight, who hunt.
From a distance you can see us moving, in miniature, across
the hills of France. This is never going to change.

That is why the cross will rise and create the last days.
We have no time to fool ourselves. We sink
beneath an us we help create. No one gets

a pass. Sam will be there singing til the end of time.
More will hear, start to find their way back home—
his crooning, a starry night, are the chords of God.

Sam Cooke's Voice

Sam Cooke's voice lets you know that heaven is possible.
So does James Baldwin's rage. All the bruised brothers,
strangest fruit hanging like earrings—Lady Day's

poplar tree. Some people just carry bigger
crosses. They define us all, as we watch crabs scuttle
along the sound of a sea (which urge proportion).

A black cross scores the road we pilgrim with penance—
though none of us deserves better than we get.
We love as if nothing depended upon it, as if

we could name our own mounting debt. Let Jesus
be the name we sing. Let our bare souls reclaim
this incline, count it as the swell of heaven. (Amid

the racial murders, the martyrs, he sings his joy
with Muhammad Ali!) It all comes back to that voice.
There's beauty here, a ship. It's nice to hear

its flapping sail, to skim the smooth wood beneath.
"A change is gonna come." "Glory hallelujah."
Every voice defines us, history in each note.

Waiting for the El
 ❧ for Paul Mariani

When God walks, lonely, do birds fall out of the sky?
Does the blue rip open a bit at its southeastern end?
His quiet sigh puts an end to a long day.

The world isn't like that, one group or another, counting
your money as theirs; though we must admit, too, that need
is kind of who we are, a sin so deep

that Augustine needed time to find it. We have Jesus's
blood on our hands. This, friend, will never change.
So we walk here as we will walk in heaven, dependent,

wrong as we, thankfully, have always been. ("Very
improvident and cheerful.") His joy must own us. Everything
we counted on will be gone. The tracks as well.

Sure, Beethoven will be able to show us some tricks
when we get there, but neither one of us will be confused.
The heavenly table, friend, has already been set.

(Cézanne will bring the circus, some beer.) Each surprise
will change us, almost set us straight, as God walks
His impossible line—down the middle of our hearts.

B Flat and Black Holes
❧ Dante's universe

How many noises shape us. Even the sun
beats wider in Dante's dance. We sing these hours
unnoticed, like carts of freshly baked bread. This includes

the verbal scuffing of winter pines, trash bins
that must be opened. A wide Alleluia is our middle
name. Dissonance, as it rights its chosen wrongs.

We're lucky our breakfast doesn't vibrate off the table!
We could come apart as well, our atoms doing
their piecemeal jag. It's the chord that makes for a clef!

The *Paradiso* speaks it; no local language could be
enough. Nor friend, but that makes sense because
we should be tension, revelation itself—all

we don't know. We go with Him, after all, on roads,
meet His people, try His trades. My brothers there know me,
look past the chaff. Chaff on my ears, on my clothes.

This poem, too, helps to complete Dante's call.
(He'll smile, pull down slightly on the badminton net,
when the after-time comes for talk, strategy, poetry.)

St. Clare of Assisi
🌿 dishes in the convent

"Usually you fish with a line, not for one," my wife notes.
(Which is why I wait!) How else do we search for our lives,
the next door? A way out of the present, more deeply in;

that fictional place where joy is a painted stage,
where St. Clare can wiggle her toes. They might be under
water, who knows; they might dictate the flow of the wind.

Who could know in a world like this? Her attitude never
needs adjusting. She rains on her own parade,
softs sheets of it, down a mountain, while lambs gambol,

define its creases. Grass heads lift here and there,
respond to the general, delicate pelt. We could build
a cabin there, but why hurry? The purples blooms

do not yet have a name. Her life sings along,
each saint going her own way; but today, we just
want her. She can teach us the grace that comes from sharing.

Half of God's vision is actually our own. Sometimes,
though, she had to put that aside, do dishes.
She spent that time populating her neighbor's face.

A Fable Begins

The night sky is clear, though blackness covers the grass,
the height of the trees. Shelves of rock have been known
to object to this usurpation, to demand more floor.

But they've been assumed, are part of a larger whole.
And the furry little woodland creatures certainly don't want
to hear that story again. (As if granite owned time.)

Squirrels like to sit in the mornings, their chins
on moss, to listen to the birds wake up the day.
They like to hear the buckeyes fall. (Or a distant

train!) The shale, barely audible, grumbles,
"I am that engine." "Oh, here we go," says a fox,
though he doesn't mind. The rocks have always provided

a bottom, the bass to their song. And the sun and clouds
provide the rest: the changing of the day, the seasons.
Rivers come into play, give us heaven. The squirrel

wishes it could sing—but the daylight, nighttime will have
to do. (Another day has just passed, and we missed it!)
"Nonsense," grumbles the rocks. "It has your voice."

"Then why do you complain," asks the busy squirrel?
"Because I'll never find my rightful home,
because the mountains never crash into the sea."

When Jesus Comes

My colleagues stock Walmart, cut me off in the aisle
at Goodwill, while my beautiful slightly autistic daughter,
oblivious, on her iPhone, walks much too closely—on my
    heels.

Such are the joys of parenthood. How can I hold it
together: as I turn a corner my Down's son has vanished!
Most days go on like this. And the real headway

they make can only be seen by a dad. That's
the clumsy joy I make my own, my thin
winter blanket. We love as badly as we can,

take consolation in that; our pushcarts are small and wobbly,
with their one bad wheel. But hey, we are all defined
by a poverty of place. We become professional Weirtonians.

Praise God for our modest reach, for our small houses.
I want to be counted among the lost at the gas station,
to die like the other old guys on my side of the street.

When Jesus comes, I want my wife to be there,
my kids to shine in their unlikely magnificent glory,
in a home whose perplexities demand an unlikely nest.

Oldest Friends

Early winter moves like the neck of a giant tortoise,
taking on more than he can, swimming on air,
one mud-foot in front of the other. You want him as pet.

But he has other ideas. Winter always likes it straight.
Like any domesticated beast, he belongs to the natural
world. You cannot change that. He embodies death.

He's rock, river. This becomes boldly evident here
as cold settles in. Your room can no longer protect you.
The heating system lags as you wear the same thick clothes.

You learn to be thankful for this. (We did not build
this house, nor make these garments!) Cold rock sings
a lovely, alien song, as we gather eons

ago, unnamed. (We only knew our own.) We were stronger
back then, our muscle against that of the beasts.
We are still much like that, and though our crosses,

statues have changed the tenor of this temporary house,
we belong to night, to this cold unconscious season.
Snow is an old friend. We pack our bags each night.

Mary
❧ the Peña Sagras

I want to sit in the dirt as someone beats
a rug again in that Garabandal alley. I don't need
anything else, just a few prophetic seeds

floating on the wind, past that stone, past the signpost
up the hill that told us where Gabriel stood. I want
to enjoy the sun there again, the Dutch person next

to me. I want the next hill over to own me.
(Or a life back in those Madonna House bean fields, where
    fleeting
friends shared chores. Life there, like one of their Byzantine

liturgies, everything changing from the outside in.)
Mary, let me hold both of your hands in mine
as we sit on any ground. Let me feel them move.

I don't need anything else. I would come to the surface
later, feel the warmth of the sun. You might even say
something, the sound of your voice, encouraging me

to lift my head. I would be the new me. I could draw
new conclusions. Maybe Linda and I could build in those
    mountains:
old people lifting stones, learning local ways.

The Waifs We Are

We bring less each time we come to the table. We'll be waifs,
what we are, at the end. Someone will have to lead us
by the hand—though that's happening now, my blind fingers

to His holy face. The contours are the moments I gather
from my children, wife: hearing her latest, her glowing
about sewing, the dresses she makes—though I'd prefer

talk about painting, music, or the time she gives
to our grandson. I've watched her. She affirms, affirms,
    delighting
him by mirroring his movements as he eats, allowing

him a babyhood. He actually grieved yesterday when he left.
It's always about that, isn't it? Each face that comes
in front of our own, we must be a road to heaven:

our lives, just like when we were kids, stacking blocks,
each new direction, a possibility. We don't know what it is
we do! Bring on the next unsolvable mystery!

We won't have a response for that one either! We sit
with Jesus, all our lives; our sorrows, the noisy crosses
we make in our little rooms, nothing for us.

On My Daughter Leaving

My daughter will leave us one day. I can feel it—the new
boyfriend come... Absence always finds another way
to make us family; our happy little party around

our dining table endures it: one loss at a time.
And so I savor the time I have left with these leave-
takers (one son already gone); I'll know something

of heaven before I come to that final door.
Bridget, David, Linda, and Jude, if you read this
down the line, know my heart beat for every diminishment,

reminder: all things must move toward their end.
(TV could never get this right.) I loved you all,
will do so then, wherever I am. You've given

me the only cup worth drinking. We know that as each
sun sets. It's like some evening ritual: each day
stealing something from itself. May this lament

outlast these winter nights. Stars don't own us.
And though saints live here, I'm glad they don't show up.
If I had more of a life, I would give that as well.

Legos and Bare Feet, Christmas Eve

Sit up straight, straighten the garbage. The biggest
moments come when you're waiting for something really
important to happen—like how you treated your brother

too early Christmas mornings. Heaven could appear
right in the middle of a childhood punch, a call
to repent, confusion. Not much changes as we age.

People irk. You fail to measure up. And still,
before you sits the crib, with its plaster straw;
you wait for completion, do the writing on the wall.

And the lights? They don't care, they twinkle again;
the *Nutcracker*, the neatly wrapped packages, as you sit,
a parent now, in the dark. It's a domestic chide,

a testament to the person you're not, whom you've never been.
Out the window, holiday lights down the street tell you
you're not alone in your failures, but part of a chorus;

a Christmas hymn from parents everywhere. This is why
we sit on uncomfortable straw. This is why we dance
over Legos, near wise men bathed in heavenly lights.

On Death

Old age doesn't catch up to you. He sits crouched,
crooked, wrinkled, in a comforter of misplaced memories.
May Sister Death rock his cradle—in the other world.

He's a knobby little character there, a fin along his spine,
with cute curled self-obsessed toes. She hymns the child,
slowly twirls, as if there were no one else in the universe.

The boy relaxes, eventually takes to wings, soon tests
the limits of the room. Death fades, as part of sunshine.
though her presence lingers. She leaves two stones by the door.

The new soul presses one to his head, then moves out
in the twilight. Older souls, in parties, populate the night
   beach.
The waves still crinkle and rise, even as they come in—

along with all the poetry in the world. Our soul
is not changed, only bettered. It loves what is human, and
   wants,
for this moment, to help staunch the pain he remembers.

His friends and family, after all, are on a different shore.
Next to it on the beach, it finds the second stone.
It looks lovely to him, quartz with mica inclusions.

For my Father-in-Law Who Once Claimed that Husbands Die First because They Want to

Let us praise older women, crowned in white.
They hold down houses, neighborhoods. Widows don't wince;
they invent the clothing that creates their station. They finish

the race, though no one watches them run. This is why
old men stand in awe. Women shoulder the more difficult
half, even as they garden, still walk the dog,

even as grandchildren gather around to find
themselves. Each deserves much more than we have given.
My wife, for example, is the most human person I know.

Each day she proceeds with a hungry zeal. It's been
a privilege to watch (to eat her food). Who else
would stand so close? Her bad jokes give life,

one which has sprung somehow out of her own.
I wouldn't trade one night out on this small town.
She's my vocation, my partner in crime. Her neuroses,

too, have schooled me: how to love. Heaven does not
waste time. And we, the old men, will wait for them,
behind others perhaps, with heavenly candy—coupons.

Mary as a Younger Girl

"Whom God loves he hides," says the hidden man,
though how could he be wrong? Flowers everywhere
unfold on time. It's like a big conspiracy.

Next thing you know it will be rain, all of us getting
a good soaking. We could wear our clown-suits out
under fronds, painted tears running down our faces.

No one would be special there. We could relax,
sit on wet rock; a few arms, the standing, opening
to heaven; no one worrying about what's next,

everything beyond us. We'd be like the rose, our springy
petals wet with answers. (We're getting closer
now.) The childlike foot has got to fall!

Perhaps Mary will come, as a younger girl, singing
in that light rain, collecting flowers. Would she be
a little pale (never in her own world)?

Would she stray from the beaten path, walk wet ferns?
You follow, though any distance makes you uncomfortable.
In every scenario she turns, owns you with love.

Winter Snow

Heaven empties—beautiful falling snow:
it visits the atmosphere. No one wants to disturb the scene
before it completes itself. That's why we don't hurry,

shovel too early—scraping cement as a team.
My Down's guy is happy to oblige. This is all the praise
we need in winter. It's a kind of triumphant shout,

this weight of white, some exercise on a cold day.
God has made us happy to be alive, soldiers
in no battle. Inside is the same. We hang up our coats,

invest in what remains to do. We look around,
heft laundry baskets, our noses still pinched in what's left
of the cold. (Too bad we're out of hot chocolate, marsh-
    mallows!)

We can look outside again. The snowfall continues.
There's a goodness to it, our lives being worked out right
in front of our eyes, being spent like a row of gold coins.

Not that they were ever worth much. A small party maybe,
a modest gathering of friends. One candle is enough.
The way it moves. The way we do, not alone.

The Apocalypse
~ COVID winter

Who would've thought it would prove so uneventful?
We move through this life in snowy boots, over-sized
clothes. We look for things to do. Did I tell you

I have a daughter! She has long hair and odd tastes
in TV. These last days keep us inside. (It's so
inconvenient!) What more can I add? My football team,

without masks, won. I took a shower, though Jesus
has always been like this: slow-hand, guiding
the blind past pubs. Let us praise Him from our tombs,

our rooms—separate, together: the strands of voices
which remain. (If He doesn't shorten the time, who
will be faithful?) Angels do the heavy lifting.

The Bible is over-sized, a chore to spring, to lift
each dusty page. (The book settles, wobbles on a disturbingly
thin neck.) The messenger's squeak might be your own.

There's no heat in our parish Cathedral, little light. Every soul
is lost until the ashy morning begins to dissolve.
Every dawn reveals, again, a spaced remnant.

Winter Guests

Jesus is a hesitant guest, someone almost
at the door. Maybe He'll bring fudge! But then again,
the pale sky doesn't need to introduce itself.

Nor do pinecones in the snow. When I hold one in my hand,
it's like the thing's a friend, as if it were made
for this moment. (It's dry fly-by-night open scales

shout "I am—and nothing else.") What other evidence
do we need? It's like those early 50s cars
in photos on the walls of Kentucky Fried on Main.

Epic black and white snows in a world without subtlety—
just after the war. (Those cumbersome machines wouldn't
    allow
for more.) I want to live then, too. For a time.

All of creation insists on our yes. Snow
is the same for everyone. It piles into lives; teaches
us gratitude, amplitude. That's in the wind, as well,

when you have to wear a hood. Everything grabs life
with both hands. Even the birds—who knows how
they sleep? Do they wake in snow caps, one eye at a time?

Advent II

Though our sins collect like old oil at the bottom of the year,
we, God's crude and dense mechanicals, still play
our parts: His grace, in mistletoe, in vexed shopping.

The happy town square Christmas tree tells you Advent
has begun, because what is good runs deeper than we
can know—in the tongues of bells, in the stone of cathedrals.

It's in a family bug, too, though no cough can change
what has to happen: the reason for the silence around
the tree—in a nearby monastery, in a late village house.

It's a night so calm now that the stars and moon, Christmas
lights, provide the speech. We move in the elevation
of the Host at midnight Mass, in the history of France,

how it comes alive, knights dismounting at a lit-up
inn, the jocular voices, heard from outside;
the spiced wine, fire warmth. Those times are framed

by holly, red berries, blessed by Clovis and Charlemagne,
the rough cross of that time; by every swain
who's ever walked the rutted snow alone.

The Last Copper

Purgatory will probably need an addition. My sin
and residue must be faced. (A string of false selves.)
Skewed Buddhist, I may have to live my life over—

in a slower motion: yes, him, and this; now her.
Who can argue at a counting table? (And so, perhaps,
my humility might grow!) I will eventually be ready.

I may have to pay the last copper. So long after I'm dead,
pray for me if you can. (I have not done well.)
Who could be consoled by this? But the long line

will be a good. There'll be joy, a measure of conviviality.
The weather will always be late spring. (We do need
our pauses!) And Jesus will show up every once in a while.

We'll be happy to be there, honestly, though I don't want to
        face
these sins again. It'll be like Confession—with a happier
crowd. (It does not matter if this is so!)

Who would not wait up for Him? Who would not
kiss His ring or construct a playhouse? I would scramble
like a bird after seed—under trees, my ridiculous sins.

Christmases

The hay is in the barn. This is what Advent's about.
Cold straw. Opinionated cattle. Still waiting on the couple.
The shepherds are about their hilly business, but why

at night? A postcard might help explain, maybe
a German folksong. We'll try to do our part.
God comes like flowers—on a sill. He hustles dead leaves.

It's why stars are so fitting; the good night is what
we always hope for. In friends, for the apocalypse. The King
reigns there—quietly for now. (My wife is nearby.)

Adult kids sleep in their rooms. You could call this happiness,
us, a little out of place. (It's what happens at Christmas.)
(This year we've taken to calling it the Advent Tree.)

My 26-year-old Downs' son has written
"Jude, go to bed," on his calendar for the twenty fourth.
Say what you will, this meekness happens every year.

Only a love that is too small to mention endures.
We'll scrape at our hearts like our car's frosted windows,
warm our hands around mugs until St. Nicholas appears.

Sterling on Black

Our world, Augustine says, is smaller when we
don't worry about others' sins. I catch them all.
I just can't help myself. Perhaps it's the badge,

or the gift of an intense inner life. I see myself
as the Lone Ranger. My horse, a Puritan Silver.
One can ride, satisfied, on a horse like that, gleam

in the sun. No one plans on being the standard.
It's the sort of thing that just happens, a momentary ring,
collected. (Heck, you hadn't even planned on the horse.)

And here you are, on a set, to the extent that one
can have one. No, God's done this: apostles,
next generation, on parade. You might feel embarrassed,

but why? What would that change? You could beat your
      breast,
never look up. You could call that humility. But your horse
deserves better. Wave! They've gathered for you.

And this is not life. There's nothing to be afraid of.
Why respell your name? You'll get off the horse at dusk.
You'll still belong to the One who's lent you all this.

Christmas Eve

The King comes to what's left of the steel mills. He takes
a left off Main because He's been here before.
He has a thousand names. That is why His streets

are so wide—though who will help us meet Him halfway?
A monk might know, but you can't find one of them
tonight, not in Weirton. This King makes His way,

though, in all things. He changes everything He touches.
His robes glisten under the moon. When God
breaks a world, there is no mistaking it. And yet,

it's ordinary. That's why Herod participates, with his shekels,
    sword,
bringing our story. It's the pain at every birth.
The tambourine jangles, not so much to honor us,

as to put us in our place. Donkeys will come down the street,
perhaps next to a police car with its blue and red lights,
as the ass makes his way through the poorer neighborhoods.

There will be campfires, rowdy shouts on the street,
one near Kentucky Fried. Everyone will know fear.
Respect will wane. But the birth still comes—once a year.

Christmas Morning

No wisemen wander these streets, at least to our knowledge.
What would they find? Stray dogs, gambling cafes.
The loneliness of the poor, what they carry for the rest of us.

Jesus was born, a cigarette hanging from His mouth.
This could be a set for a movie, but it's really happening
again. An old man is grumbling, making noise

looking into a garbage can. "They come on Tuesday,"
part of you wants to say. (Angels have heard it
on high.) This is how it is everywhere. Too much space

between people. It's like everyone's outside downtown, eating
distracted dinners on paper plates. There's nowhere
to put the waste. We prefer things this way. It's honest.

The friend you make is for the moment, might speak
a foreign language. It all fits because nothing does.
We are pilgrims here, of a sort. (We all wanted toy trains

for Christmas as youths. Now we've gotten them.)
There's a glory in this: the sound of a slightly feckless
car up Main Street, its wheels leaving rubber behind.

The Seafarer

What is his ocean to me? The rolling pendulum,
a physical truth too big to ignore? Maybe
if I lived there, soaked high at the mast, out

in the middle of the North Sea. But here it's Tuesday,
and it's time to take out the recyclables, to look for a chance
to take a right at the red light. We don't have time

for perspective. Or maybe that's all we have. Because nothing
matters as much as this creaking mast, this Ring-giver.
We need to be careful about the cliffs, the mists.

We only have this family, friend, a hyphenated
comitatus. That and a will to plumb the sea rises.
Our winters here are an icy hail-scur, a poverty;

they're an unspectacular storm we find in the kitchen.
Our lives are riddled by Anglo-Saxon scops.
Our horned helmets crowd the dining room table.

In the meanwhile I clip my toenails with industrial clippers.
The bathroom may not seem much like a Northern longship,
but hoary heads face the mirror, learn how to keen.

December 26ᵗʰ, Feast Day
❧ after Greene's *The Power and the Glory*

Snow and cold, the wind like it has something against you:
we grew up in stuff like this, though my parents had harder
stories yet. They might also be true, though I doubt that.

Snow's like it's always been. Tall tales make winter
ours. It stokes our imaginations, schools us, like cinnamon
in eggnog. We can finally become who we really are;

we can stretch our legs with the best of them, and saunter—
one of those things every kid longs to master.
(How else are you supposed to get through these winters?)

Using a lasso comes next, maybe some calf-roping;
we'll rewrite Alban Butler's tepid *Lives of the Saints*,
screw them up into something proper, fitting.

Who'd follow a saint if all he did was suffer,
probably through years of silence? No, we need
to give 'em spurs for the walking—bow-legged—a saddle,

so bright they never have to introduce themselves.
Brother, walk with me and the sun will shine
as she was meant to do—on cowpokes like us.

Negative One, Snow and Wind

Morning's like an obliviously cold engine running
outside your door. Surely no horse would respond
were you to call out through the blizzard to Nebraska's barn.

(Nobody minds death. It's the getting there that stops us.
It's like you're dreaming poker and you can never get
that fifth card.) The world clamps shut with the freeze, a shell

tightly sealed. So this day demands a run-up:
a hot shower, Christmas cologne, the elliptical downstairs
with my son. And then, in time, we go outside.

God unveils our lives, each necessary step. We don't
have to know where we are going, and how could we?
We're strangers in this house, if we know it or not—a recurring

satisfaction. "I think I'll make a bologna sandwich."
These are the joys we get! Sunny climes. The One
who loves us is never wrong. Halfway there

is halfway from here. And a sandwich takes you back to child-
    hood,
when you didn't care so much about what happened next.
Some moments were races to find the next place to go.

Marconi and What He Had for Lunch
➤ Vernel Bagneris, Youtube

When it rains, it rains pennies from Vernel's heaven.
Of course, we never see that, all the glitter.
(At every university, no one ever gets enough respect!)

But it's there, friend, right where it's always been.
(This Christmas at my place everyone likes the small mega-
    phone;
It blurts and distorts their voice, as we always do.)

It's the good urge that counts, the music, a dancing,
glimmerings after Marconi. How much sweeter life is when we
see the graced incompleteness of other people!

It's like no one's read the directions on how to live.
It's like Jesus has given us just enough to get along.
How else would we be able to, get along, that is?

Wish I could say I'll do better, though I suspect
I will. Heaven is probably filled with yokels
who started (and will finish) like me. Heck, they all

came from a mother's pain; none of them having
too many answers. We just have to keep on plugging—
enough holes to make our horn, the sweetest music.

PART II

Billy Collins Walks into
Walmart to Buy Some Herbicide

My Wife is the Only Person
I really Know

Everyone else just drops by.

I know how she rises, how she settles in.
She's transformed our mid-block brick house
into exhibition space, has scattered
wild seeds from the Neolithic:
larkspur and columbine,
into a large stone circle out front.
She's a butterfly, has been spooked by them;
She takes each room with enthusiasm—
no matter what I'm reading!

(It was clear even then—on monkey bars,
in red tennis shoes. Here was someone
I would be a fool to lose tract of.)

Our orbits waver, though she is clearly
more generous than I: three neighborly women
she's walked dogs with; the young artist
and mother next door,
anyone at the supermarket.

She's clean, less orderly than I,
a woman with a plan: freeze-dried food
stacked in the basement, every empty box,
saved. She yips when I, a cabbie, unable
to shake my loose, turn, back right wheel
over the curb. Her loud laugh—she's

a fireman's daughter— defines us, as does
her imaginative prayer: she and John of the Cross,
Jesus and Mary on folding chairs.
And though I fall shorter than she in many ways,
which of us, at this point, would apologize
for who we are?

Our failures keep us running—
at wrong angles.

It's how we'll get to heaven.

Northern Folk

Winter offers a world with fewer options;
the house can hardly breathe in this cold.
The body—its walls—creak, give;
like an old man, upstairs, coughing in bed,
his bedsprings, violating each task.

If you must leave your house this morning,
if you make it out to your vehicle,
you've got a chance. Here you are defined
by your scraper.

Of course, the inside of the car
changes things, all the promising knobs!

Life becomes a battle of climes.

Sloth can't survive this far north,
as cold gives way begrudgingly—
with an abstract, metallic, icy screech;
from the time you leave your car, until
you get your back door open again.
This is why there's such a cut in northern voices.
No one here has time to dally. Get to the heat,
the warm bread, butter of things!

Northern people can-do.
The more they know snow, the quicker they hello.
These people still write letters, build fires;
but they know, too, that any talk in the cold

is a wind-down, a way to ease
into warmer company.

Northern people appreciate brute beauty:
shale, any cold rock that impales the air,
that doesn't care a whit about you or me.
Northern folk like the dig in streams
on days when waters flow; they like the dirt rut
in each: goshawks screaming, swooping—
the blunt edge of brightening mornings.

They like to learn the names of things.

Frozen Poem

You rumble, walk inside the furnace—
huge metal sleeves.
Small animals might be hiding in here,
bits of their skeletons.

This is what your life has become,
a trundle down industrial-sized metal casings,
echoes, as you search for warmth,
primal heat, flint; what you find
are old newspapers.

You spend too much time here.

The thin doubling sound, your feet,
they almost sustain you: it's a kind of promise—
though not enough to matter much.
It's like every other saving bit of this world.
Like the strength you've shown up until now,
how it works you up and into something.

Saints have done this kind of thing forever.
You are in their company,

icy sleeves next to new fires.

Tin Soldiers

They line up briskly beneath the Advent tree,
having formed a sodality: "Knights of our Lady
and of the Coming Christmas Lights."
And though they play squeaky cards
when at ease, their tin hats (with some effort)
turned backwards, they understand order,
propriety. You could trust your daughter
to one, were she small enough.

Alas, life seldom goes in that direction:
childhood walnuts, ginger creams, the huge
navel orange I always found in my stocking.
This does not deter them.
They could tell you tales, all true,
about their snowy Russian campaign in 1812.
They know about strategic retreats, supply lines,
not to mention gingerbread fairies.

They've been called on ever since, always
at Christmas. Sugar plums do not dull their resolve.
Nor do the cars gliding by, their snow-lights,
outside your window. (Neighbors do what they can,
string lights, variations on the crèche scene.)

Carolers from other times sing the season.

One snow brings other falls to mind.
A baby is being born, and must always be.

Sister Death as Donkey

She comes, a small one,
bells in her pierced ears.
You probably won't notice her at first.
One moment she'll just be there,
shambling alongside, like she's always
been your Sancho. And talk!
She'll probably be in the middle of a sentence,
though if you need to sit,
she will know—provide sandals.
She's diminutive, true, but strong;
she remembers every scrape in your life.

She has a heart for sin.

Death understands, knows
that this is new country for you—
like her first trip to the Holy Land.
Next time, she says, she wants to come
as a camel: the rising up-jerk—
it surprises—and then that long and
slightly goofy lope. It would be worth it,
don't you think? (Though she wonders,
would that effect conversation?)

You'll notice small tambourine zills,
which now rim her blanket. She has
many small animal friends,
thought of bringing a few—
flowers to vase your passage.
She knows jokes, is happy to share

a few, locally specific. (She's written, she says,
several books on the subject.)

The ride itself will take as long
as you'd like. She's always
ready to pray—will help you gather
your past if you want to,
might offer saddlebag peanuts.
She might even sing you a Peruvian
folk song, one with a slight
regional waver in her voice.

You like death.

(She knows.)

A canteen with small wings appears.

She asks after your mother, father,
names off your childhood friends.
She remembers something nice about each.
Walking now, slightly in front of her,
you'll notice the tattooed heart
on her right shin. She's hung out,
she says, with all sorts of people.

This take—granted—comes from
the other side, where things are better,
though I really don't see
how that matters.

Tunisia

It just sounds nice, doesn't it?
Warm in the evenings, clothing, light,
but layered, to fit the climate.
Most pedestrians would be local;
a few small cars. My wife would love
the open-air markets. My Down's guy,
he would take to natives.
(He'd be gone for hours!)

Tunisia would not exactly be heaven,
though Jesus might show up, waving
like a minor politician to friends
as He walks down the street.

Water would be cool
right out of the well, a beautiful large
ceramic chipped cup on a chain.
At nights when we sit on the roof
everybody would be friendly,
ready to comment on constellations,
types of breezes, the fireworks.

There would be sport in Tunisia,
though most of that on dusty streets,
barefoot young boys, shouting
their kind of praise. There would be nice
outdoor tables where we could share
beers or the lives of the saints,
passages, with passers-by.

People, quiet, like desert flowers,
would always be ready for a joke.

There might be some other side
to Tunisia, but that would be
for another day—a day where neither
flowers nor vases would grace the tables,
a day filled with wind and grey:
passing clouds, curtains waving outside
the windows, all of that, a remnant
from some past age.

Your Welcome

I've never wanted a St. Bernard.
They are much too big, and I wouldn't
want to be tasked with refilling that cask.
Or too many parrots. I wouldn't want that either.

Of course, you would be welcome.
If I had beer, I'd offer, or we could go get some.
I could show you the holy parts of the college
like I generally do for visiting writers.

You don't have to be one of them.

If you were a Catholic we could talk about that,
about Jesus and what He's doing in both of our lives.
(Talk always seems to go in its own direction.)

With writers I have to keep one eye on the time,
though we needn't do that with you.

By now we might be talking about your kids,
or mine; Linda would suggest a walk
to the neighborhood park like she usually does.
If you need a place to crash, we could offer you
a couch or extended time on a basement cot,
like we once did for an artist friend.

You'd have to watch our coon-bird dog
mix though; every night at eight he gets pretty crazy.
He likes to tear around, under the dining table,

and then into the living room, where he bounds
onto the couch, full speed, a chew toy
in his ready mouth. He rides that sofa,
repeatedly, smack against the wall.
(We must play, chase him!)

Also, zip up your chaired pockets. He is a furry thief.

I think he'd do well on a farm, deer to chase—
or to run with—though we would temper that
with you here.

In My "Forgiveness" Prayer Room

My parents are tube people, giant skydancers,
the kind you see flapping next to used car dealerships.
They extend high above my slightly elevated floor,
the two comfortable seats—after you dodder
through the fun house rails to the right, steps
removed from its distorting mirrors, air hoses,
perspective-denying floors and walls.
(The front of the house is my huge face;
its door, my clown mouth.)

I dreamed the two of them flapped outside yesterday,
in the darkness for some reason, collapsing, rising,
their arms deflating, then snapping back
toward attention under (I want it to have been there)
the moon. They lived difficult lives.

Those times were real, before they had me.
They died, like all of us, a hundred times
before it mattered, sometimes feeling like Lear,
after his cliff, sometimes like his fool.
They fell young, and aged—just God and them.

I'd never really given that much thought.
For me, they were mostly the people, parents,
who came up short, whatever their pain.

(Our feelings are like giant ganglia that grow
on and in their own juices, aren't they, measuring
us and everyone else?)

I want to spend more time with them
in those deadly moments. I want to flap, snap
in that dark breeze, my plastic, folding self-consciously
onto itself—the momentary despair that slight
weight increase can bring; how they
would then fight to air-right themselves
against the night, the tall trees. They had to wonder,
would they make it, would they hold up,
the material they were, buoyed by bad air?
They had to have tried, again, almost against
their will because that was how they were made.

They couldn't exactly remove themselves,
go anywhere, could they? They had to finish
what they started. They cried out often, but
to whom, and what could they say? Perhaps it was
August, 1942, and they were in a war, or later,
alone with eight children in some cheap room
that needed paint: little food, no vacation pay.

Who was there to understand *them*?
Did the Confessional screen close too quickly?
Was everything by some book?

They had to have limped home like all of us.

Maybe it was 1947, and I wasn't born yet.
It doesn't matter anymore, except in the lives
of their children, grandchildren. Those of us
here now live scattered lives, almost trees ourselves.
Most of what we have in this world,
we've gotten from them. And I'm grateful for that.

My heart still sounds, beats in and out; my own
children, grandchild, are miracles. I would
stay forever to help them. I would sit
in my parents' garden, on the ground; I would sing
a song on a cheap guitar. Nothing changes.
God still lives in His heaven, in spent
winter plants, in the chill. It's good that something
larger than us runs things. The bigger canvas
means we don't understand. Dig with me, grandma,
grandpa, dig with me, all of you.
They will certainly need our help.

CPSIA information can be obtained
at www.ICGtesting.com
Printed in the USA
BVHW072025201121
622061BV00003B/15

9 781621 387848